COUNTRYWISE

GERMANY
AND GERMAN

Janine Amos

Chrysalis Children's Books

Contents

This edition published in 2003 by
Chrysalis Children's Books
64 Brewery Road, London N7 9NT

Copyright © Chrysalis Books PLC

Edited by Nicola Wright
Designed by Kate Buxton
Additional illustration by Guy Smith
Consultants Michael Hirst, Jonathan Wrigh
Cover design by Keren Orr-Greenfeld

A CIP catalogue record for this book is available
from the British Library

ISBN 184138 476 3

Printed in China
10 9 8 7 6 5 4 3 2 1

About this book

In this book you can find out about Germany – its people, landscapes and language. For example, discover what the Germans like to eat and drink, what they do for a living, and what famous German places look like.

Where Germany is in the world

North America

South America

Europe

Asia

Africa

Australia

Find out, also, what school days are like for German children, and about their holidays and festivals. On page 26 there is a special section to introduce you to speaking German.

Hello!

Guten Tag!

It explains how to use and pronounce everyday words and phrases, so you can make friends and ask for things in cafés and shops. Also, some German words and their meaning are given throughout the book to help you increase your vocabulary.

Map of Germany

Germany shares borders with nine other European countries: Denmark, Poland, Czechoslovakia, Austria, Switzerland, France, Luxembourg, Belgium and the Netherlands.

Longest river:
The Rhine, 1,320 kilometres. It flows from Switzerland to the North Sea. The Rhine is a busy waterway, with barges carrying goods up and down the river. There are many castles along its banks.

die Karte
map

der Fluß*
river

Highest mountain:
Zugspitze, Alps, 2,968 metres. You can ride to the top by mountain train and cable car to see the spectacular views.

der Berg
mountain

North Sea

Netherlands

Dortmund
Essen
Düsseldorf
Cologne
Bonn

Belgium

Rhine

Luxembourg

Rhineland
Palatinc

Saarla

France

* The German letter **ß** is pronounced like the double **s** in the English word *class*.

4

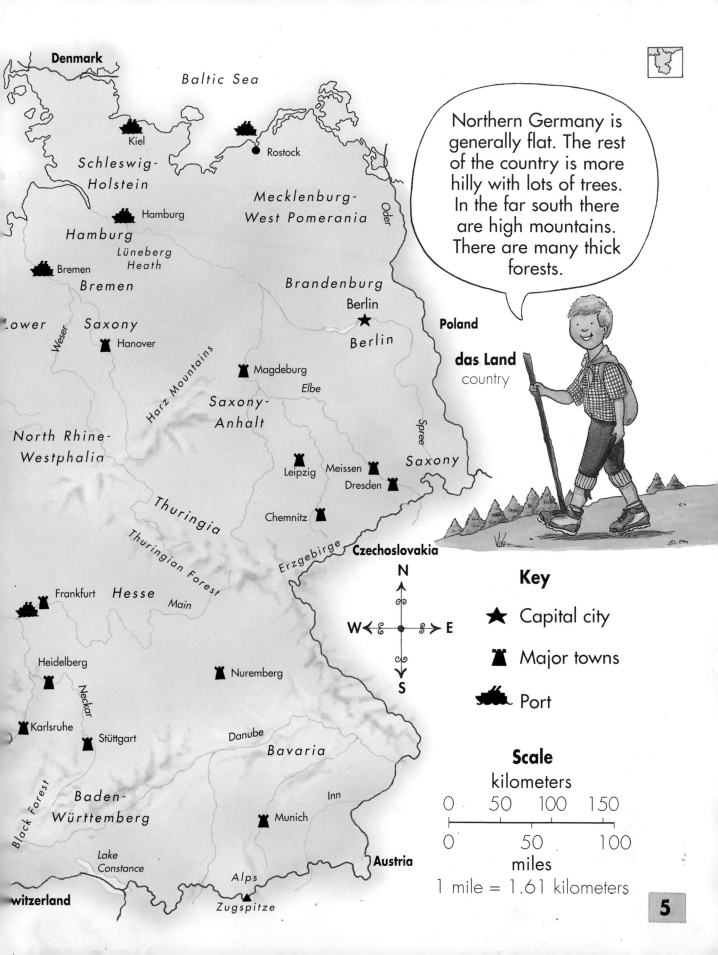

Denmark

Baltic Sea

Kiel

Rostock

Schleswig-
Holstein

Mecklenburg-
West Pomerania

Oder

Hamburg

Hamburg

Lüneberg
Heath

Bremen

Bremen

Brandenburg

Berlin

★

Berlin

Poland

Lower

Saxony

Weser

Hanover

Magdeburg

Elbe

Saxony-
Anhalt

Spree

das Land
country

Harz Mountains

North Rhine-
Westphalia

Leipzig

Meissen

Saxony

Dresden

Thuringia

Chemnitz

Thuringian Forest

Erzgebirge

Czechoslovakia

Frankfurt

Hesse

Main

Heidelberg

Neckar

Nuremberg

Karlsruhe

Stüttgart

Danube

Bavaria

Black Forest

Baden-
Württemberg

Inn

Munich

Lake
Constance

Alps

Switzerland

Zugspitze

Austria

Northern Germany is generally flat. The rest of the country is more hilly with lots of trees. In the far south there are high mountains. There are many thick forests.

Key

★ Capital city

♜ Major towns

⛴ Port

Scale

kilometers

0   50   100   150

0   50   100

miles

1 mile = 1.61 kilometers

5

Facts about Germany

Between 1945 and 1990 Germany was split into two different countries, West Germany and East Germany. They were reunited in 1990. Now Germany is one of the largest and most powerful European countries.

Size:
357,039 sq km

Population:
79 million

This has been the West German flag since 1949. It is now used by the unified Germany.

die Fahne
flag

The Head of State is the President. However, it is the Chancellor (rather like a Prime Minister in Britain) who leads the government of the country.

Official name:
Bundesrepublik Deutschland (Federal Republic of Germany)

Capital city:
Berlin

Language

The official language is German, though people speak it differently throughout the country.

die Sprache
language

Plattdeutsch (which means 'flat German'), is the dialect spoken in the lowlands of the north.

Hochdeutsch is the standard form of German.

Money

 The currency used in Germany is the euro.

Germany is not the only country to use euros. On January 1 2002, twelve countries in Europe began to use euro notes and coins. All euros can be used in any of those twelve countries.

 One euro can be split into 100 cents. Coins are made in amounts of 1 and 2 euros and 1, 2, 5, 10, 20 and 50 cents. Notes are made in amounts of 5, 20, 50, 100, 200, and 500 euros.

das Geld
money

Some things made in Germany

Autos und Motorräder
cars and motorbikes
BMW, Volkswagen, Mercedes-Benz

der Wein
wine
Liebfraumilch, Bernkasteler

Eisen und Stahl
iron and steel
(*produced mainly in the Ruhr valley*)

das Bier
beer
Export, Pils, Bock

Elektrogeräte
electrical goods
Bosch, Braun

Regions of Germany

Germany has a varied landscape with low, flat plains, steep river valleys and wooded mountains. In the south, the high Alps are covered with snow for several months every year.

The flat, green land in the north is dotted with windmills and thatched cottages.

Winters are usually cold in Germany, and the summers hot. In the mountains, the weather is cooler and wetter.

The northern coast is popular for sailing and other water sports. Nature reserves protect the many sea birds.

das Naturschutzgebiet
nature reserve

Holiday makers on the sandy beaches shelter from the wind in special beach baskets.

The Lüneburg Heath, south of Hamburg, is an area of great natural beauty. In summer purple heather covers the ground. Part of the heath is a nature reserve, where there are wild boar, red deer and otters.

der Wald
forest

The forests of the Harz Mountains in the middle of the country are the perfect magical setting for famous German fairy tales, such as Hansel and Gretel.

Along the Elbe River in eastern Germany you can see spectacular pillars of rock rising from the forests. People like to climb them.

There are many coalfields in the north-west and east of Germany. Factories that produce iron and steel have been built in the same areas because they use lots of coal.

In north-eastern Germany there are many lakes and woodlands. It is an ideal place for camping, hiking, sailing and fishing.

The Mosel River twists through a steep-sided valley. The slopes are lined with vineyards.

The southern region of Bavaria is famous for its picturesque churches and castles. People go skiing and sledging in the Bavarian Alps during the winter. In summer they go there to climb, to walk among the wild flowers or simply to admire the views.

There are large industrial cities and towns all over the country. Frankfurt, on the River Main, is a major German commercial, industrial and cultural centre.

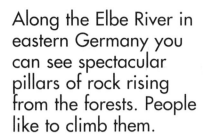

Berlin

Berlin is Germany's capital. It is a lively city holding many concerts, plays and art exhibitions. There's always something exciting to see.

The ruins of Kaiser-Wilhelm-Gedächtniskirche (a Memorial Church) have been left as a monument to the bombing. A modern church and tower have been built beside it.

Berlin was badly damaged by bombs in World War II. A lot of the city had to be rebuilt.

The Kurfürstendamm (shortened to Ku'damm) is Berlin's busy central avenue. The street is lined with trees. Here people shop, visit the art galleries and theatres, or sit outside cafés watching the street entertainers.

Berlin has more parks and woodland than any other European city. The Tiergarten is an area of parkland in the centre of the city. Historical monuments stand among the trees.

Memorial to the Berlin Airlift in 1948–1949

There are sandy beaches along the east bank of Berlin's Havel River. Wannsee, the biggest beach, is a perfect place to sunbathe and watch the many sailing boats on the water.

Famous Famous buildings and monuments

The Reichstag
(parliament building)

Brandenburg Gate
(a huge, stone arch, built 200
years ago in the centre of Berlin)

Philharmonie
(home of the famous Berlin
Philharmonic Orchestra)

Alexanderplatz
(where a huge clock shows the
time in cities all over the world)

Schloß Charlottenburg
(built 300 years ago as a summer
palace for Queen Sophie Charlotte.
Today it is a museum)

Siegessäule
(Victory Column)

Fernsehturm
(the 365 metre high
television tower)

You can
travel about easily
on the city's U-Bahn
(underground railway)
and trams.

In a typical German town

Many German towns have a shopping precinct where cars aren't allowed. It is a pleasant place to shop, with trees, benches and cafés.

der Laden
shop

die Kirche
church

das Rathaus
town hall

das Reisebüro
tourist office

das Café
café

dia Imbißstube
snack bar

der Supermarkt
supermarket

die Bank
bank

die Bäckerei
bakery

der Markt
market

German shops are usually open from 8 or 9 am until 6 pm. On Saturdays they close at 12 or 1 pm – but on the first Saturday in the month they are open in the afternoon too.

Almost every town has a market day each week. At a market you can buy fruit, flowers, vegetables, herbs, eggs, meat, cheese, fish and bread.

die Polizei
police

die Apotheke
chemist

das Postamt
post office

das Lebensmittelgeschäft
grocery shop

die Konditorei
cake shop and café

die Buchhandlung
bookshop

die Fußgängerzone
pedestrian precinct

Eating in Germany

People enjoy their food and drink in Germany. Each region has its own specialities. The country is well known for its sausages and bread. There are many kinds to choose from.

A traditional German breakfast (Frühstuck) includes a selection of breads with ham, sausage and cheese as well as jam and honey. Some people have a boiled egg too.

Children like to drink hot chocolate.

die heiße Schokolade
hot chocolate

Half way through the morning, some Germans have a sandwich snack.

In the afternoons people like to visit their friends, or go to a Konditorei, to eat cake and drink coffee.

Lunch (Mittagessen) is the main meal of the day in many parts of Germany. It is often a large dish of pork or veal with vegetables.

Some typical German dishes

die Käsespätzle
cheese noodles

der Kartoffelpuffer
potato pancake

die Bratwürste
grilled chipolatas

die Linsensuppe
lentil soup

der Apfelstrudel
apple strudel

**die Schwarzwälder
Kirschtorte**
Black Forest gateau

das Sauerkraut
pickled cabbage

Drink

der Wein
wine
*Sekt, Piesporter,
Bernkasteler*

das Bier
beer
*Bock
Pils
Weißbier*

die Berliner Weiße
(fizzy beer
with syrup)

der Schnaps
spirits
*Himbeergeist
Kirschwasser*

The evening meal (Abendbrot)
is often light. It might be a
selection of cheeses and cold
meats with different varieties
of bread and salad. This is
usually followed by fresh fruit.

der Kartoffelsalat
potato salad

die Weißwürte
white sausages

What people do

Some people in Germany work as farmers or in forestry. Many more have jobs in industry, and there are factories throughout the country.

There are many fishermen on the northern coasts. Fish are caught with huge nets and frozen immediately onboard the fishing boats.

der Fischer
fisherman

die Fabrik
factory

The main wine-producing areas are in the Rhine and the Mosel valleys.

Steel mills in the Ruhr region produce most of the country's steel. Factories turn it into cars, trucks, ships and machinery.

Farmers grow potatoes and cereals, such as wheat, barley, rye and oats. Many keep dairy cows and pigs.

Hops are grown in Bavaria to make beer.

Germany produces many optical instruments, including cameras and binoculars.

Germany's chemical industry produces important drugs and medicines.

Woodworking is a traditional craft in the forests. Cuckoo clocks are made in the Black Forest. Wooden toys are also popular and are a speciality of the Erzgebirge in the east.

das Holz
wood

Wood, especially pine, beech and oak, is an important product in Germany. The forests and sawmills employ many people.

In the Alps, lots of people work in hotels and sports centres which are used by tourists.

der Skilehrer
ski-instructor

Children in Germany

Here you can find out something about school life in Germany, and how children spend their time.

Many schools in Germany start early in the day at 8 am. In the winter months it is still dark when children leave their homes.

School finishes early, by 1 pm. Many children go home for a big lunch and then do their homework in the afternoons. Some children spend their afternoons at daycare centres until their parents return from work.

die Kinder
children

Children begin school in Germany at the age of six. At the end of each year they get a school report. If their marks are bad they have to stay in the same class for another year. After four years of primary school, children go on to different secondary schools.

die Schule
school

18

On their first day at primary school children are given a big cone of sweets.

das Kind
child

Some schools give sport, music or craft lessons after lunch.

Skilaufen
skiing

When it snows, children take sledges to parks or hillsides. In the winter holidays many children go skiing with their families. In the summer they go walking or cycling.

die Schulferien
school holidays

Sport and outdoor activities are very popular in Germany. Many schools teach swimming, football and tennis.

der Sport
sport

History of Germany

A.D. 962

King Otto of Germany became the first emperor of a huge area of land in western and central Europe. It became known as the Holy Roman Empire. The large empire was very powerful but difficult to rule. The emperor was often challenged by noblemen and princes.

1517

A German monk called Martin Luther spoke out against the teachings of the Roman Catholic church. The people who supported Luther were called Protestants.

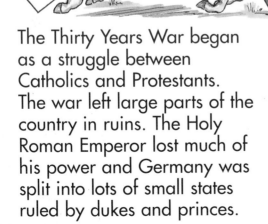

1618

The Thirty Years War began as a struggle between Catholics and Protestants. The war left large parts of the country in ruins. The Holy Roman Emperor lost much of his power and Germany was split into lots of small states ruled by dukes and princes.

1871

Prussia was the largest state. A Prussian leader, Otto von Bismarck, brought together the German states to form the new, powerful German Empire. Wilhelm I became the first German emperor.

Germany was defeated in World War I by the Allies, including France, Britain and the USA. The people were poor and hungry. People joined with the army to rebel against the emperor. He left for Holland, and Germany became a republic. The German people chose their own government.

In the 1930s millions of people were very poor and without work. In 1933 Adolf Hitler came to power. He was the leader of the Nazi Party and he promised to find work for everyone. However, the Nazis persecuted their opponents and Germans who were Jewish. Hitler also wanted to conquer the whole of Europe. In 1939 Germany invaded Poland and World War II began.

1940s

The war ended in 1945 when the Allies defeated Germany. The country was divided into four zones. In 1949 three of these zones joined to become West Germany. The fourth zone became East Germany. The city of Berlin was split into two.

A wall was built right through Berlin. People were separated from their families and friends.

1989

The Berlin wall was pulled down. In 1990 Germany celebrated its unification – it had become one country again.

Famous places

Many thousands of tourists from all over the world visit Germany every year. There are lots of beautiful and interesting places to see. Here are some of them:

The Baltic Sea coast has some popular seaside resorts. In summer the beaches are crowded with beach baskets. Windsurfing and sailing are favourite sports.

der Strand
beach

The town of Hamelin was made famous by the tale of the Pied Piper, who cleared the town of a plague of rats. He then led all the children away too, charming them with his magic flute.

The wine-producing town of Meissen stands on the Elbe River. A cathedral and a castle look down over the town. At the porcelain factory visitors can watch the famous china being made.

Potsdam is an area of parks and woodland close to Berlin. You can visit Sanssouci Palace with its magnificent terraced gardens. The palace was designed for King Frederick II in 1745, from the king's own sketches.

The gigantic cathedral attracts many visitors to the city of Cologne. Inside the cathedral there is a golden shrine. It is said to contain the bones of the Three Kings who visited Jesus when he was born.

The old university town of Heidelberg is on the banks of the River Neckar.

The Black Forest attracts thousands of visitors who enjoy walking in the beautiful countryside. The forest's name comes from the dark colour of its pine trees.

The heart of Munich is the Marienplatz. People gather in the square opposite the town hall to see the figures of the 43-bell Glockenspiel acting out scenes from German history.

der Schloß
castle

Linderhof castle was also built by King Ludwig.

Neuschwanstein castle in Bavaria is one of Germany's most famous fairy-tale castles. It was built for King Ludwig II.

Many visitors go boating on the Königsee lake in Bavaria to admire St Bartholomäu church with the mountains in the background.

der See
lake

Festivals

There are many festivals and celebrations throughout the year in Germany. They take place in the big cities and in the countryside too. Almost every town and village has its own fair. Beer and wine tents are put up in the marketplace and a band plays.

Carnival (Fasching) is a time of fun and feasting in February, just before Lent. It is celebrated in many parts of Germany. In Cologne, there is a famous fancy-dress procession through the town. Traditionally the festival was held to drive away the dark spirits of winter and to welcome in the spring.

der Fasching
carnival

Passion plays are presented in some towns at Easter, showing the last days of Christ on earth. The oldest is the passion play at Oberammergau, which takes place every ten years.

Visitors from all over the world come to the large festival in Munich, called the Oktoberfest. People dress up in traditional costume. Men wear leather trousers (Lederhosen) and women wear embroidered dresses (Dirndl) with aprons.

In the autumn, farmers in Bavaria bring their cattle down from the mountains to spend the cold winter indoors. The cows are decorated with flowers and you can hear the echo of their cowbells across the valleys.

das Fest
festival

On the night of 5 December St Nicholas, or Santa Claus, comes to hide little presents in children's shoes. His scary servant, Ruprecht, carries a stick to beat naughty children!

St Martin's Day on 11 November is a children's festival. Children carry paper lanterns on sticks, which they have made at school.

Germans celebrate Christmas on Christmas Eve. People exchange presents and go to church.

New Year's Eve is a special time in Germany. At midnight the churchbells ring and people set off fireworks in every town and village. Children are often allowed to stay up and join in the celebrations.

Speaking German

You will find lots of useful German words on the following pages, along with some simple phrases to help you to ask for things.

You will see that every word is written in three different ways:

these are the German words

this gives you an idea of how to say the words

this is what it means in English

ein Orangensaft
(eye-n oranjensaft)
an orange juice

In each speech bubble you will find a German phrase, a guide to pronouncing it, and its English meaning. You will see how easy it is to go shopping or to order what you want to eat and drink at a café.

Ich möchte ein Eis
(Ikh murkta eye-n Ice)
I would like an ice-cream

the German words

how to pronounce the German words

the English translation

Making friends

Here are some simple phrases to use when you want to make friends in Germany.

Ja
(*Yah*)
Yes

Bitte
(*Bitta*)
Please

Guten Tag
(*Gooten Targ*)
Hello

Tut mir leid
(*Toot meer light*)
I'm sorry

Herr
(*Hair*)
Mr

Fräulein
(*Froi-line*)
Miss

Hallo. Wie heißt du?
(*Hallo. Vee highst doo?*)
Hello. What is your name?

Ich heiße Karin. Und du?
(*Ikh highsa Kareen. Unt doo?*)
My name is Karen. And yours?

Wo verbringst du deine Ferein?
(*Vo fair-bringst doo diner fairy-en?*)
Where are you spending your holiday?

Ich wohne da drüben.
(*ikh vone-a dah drewben.*)
I live over there.

Wie alt bist du?
(*Vee alt bist doo?*)
How old are you?

Ich bin zwölf.
(*Ikh bin tsverlf.*)
I am twelve.

Nein
(*Nine*)
No

Danke
(*Danka*)
Thank you

Auf Wiedersehen
(*Owf veeder-zayen*)
Goodbye

Entschuldigung
(*Ent-shuldigung*)
Excuse me

Frau
(*Frow*)
Mrs

Sprechen Sie Englisch?
(*Shprekhen zee en-glish?*)
Do you speak English?

27

At the café

ein Eisbecher
(*eye-n ice-becker*)
an ice-cream sundae

einen Apfelsaft
(*eye-nen apfelsaft*)
apple juice

eine heiße Schokolade
(*eye-na hicer Shokolarda*)
a hot chocolate

die Karte
(*dee karta*)
menu

eine Bratwurst
(*eye-na bratvorst*)
a fried sausage

ein Glas
(*eye-n glass*)
a glass

Here are some people ordering food and drink at a café. They are using the words **Ich möchte**, which mean **I would like**. Using this simple phrase you can order any of the items around the picture.

Was möchten Sie?
(Vass murkten zee?)
What can I get you?

Ich möchte ein belegtes Brötchen mit Schinken und einen Orangensaft, bitte.
(Ikh murkta eye-n belaygtas brertkhen mit shinken unt eye-nen oranjensaft, bitta.)
I would like a ham sandwich and an orange juice, please.

ein belegtes Brötchen mit Schinken
(*eye-n belaygtas brertkhen mit shinken*)
an open ham sandwich

einen Orangensaft
(*eye-nen oranjensaft*)
an orange juice

ein Erdbeereis
(*eye-n airt-bair-ice*)
a strawberry ice cream

 ein Vanilleeis
(*eye-n vaniya-ice*)
a vanilla ice cream

ein gemischter Salat]
(*eye-n gemishter salart*)
a mixed salad

Ich möchte ein Eis, bitte.
(Ikh murkta eye-n ice, bitta.)
I would like an ice-cream, please.

eine Cola
(*eye-na Cola*)
a Coca-Cola

**Welche Sorte –
Erdbeere, Vanille oder Schokolade?**
(Welkkha zorta – airt-bair, vaniya oder shokolarda?)
Which flavour – strawberry, vanilla or chocolate?

Salz und Pfeffer
(*zalts unt pfeffer*)
salt and pepper

Herr Ober! Die Rechnung, bitte.
(Hair oba! Dee rekhnung, bitta.)
Waiter! The bill, please.

die Rechnung
(*dee reknung*)
the bill

 eine Portion Pommes frites
(*eye-na portsee-on pomme frit*)
some chips

Käsekuchen
(kayza-kookhen)
cheesecake

At the shops

Bonbons
(*bonbons*)
sweets

Honig
(*hoan-ikh*)
honey

Kartoffeln
(*kartoffeln*)
potatoes

Eier
(*eye-yer*)
eggs

Milch
(*milkh*)
milk

Birnen
(*beer-nen*)
pears

Kirsche
(*kirscher*)
cherries

The children are shopping for fruit (Obst) and vegetables (Gemüse) at a grocery shop (Lebensmittelgeschäft). Around the picture are some useful words for things you might want to buy, using the same phrase **Ich möchte.**

Darf ich Ihnen helfen?
(*Darf ikh eenen helfen?*)
Can I help you?

Ich möchte ein Kilo Äpfel.
(*Ikh murkta eye-n kilo epfel.*)
I'd like a kilo of apples.

Kuchen
(*kookhen*)
cake

ein Huhn
(*eye-n hoon*)
chicken

ein Kohlkopf
(*eye-n coal-kopf*)
a cabbage

Wurst
(*voorst*)
sausage

ein Buch
(*eye-n bookh*)
a book

Briefmarken
(*breefmarken*)
stamps

Brot
(*broat*)
bread

Wieviele möchten Sie?
(*Vee-feela murkten zee?*)
How many would you like?

Zehn Eier, bitte.
(*Tsayn eye-yer, bitta.*)
Ten eggs, please.

Pflaumen
(*pflowmen*)
plums

Kekse
(*keksa*)
biscuits

Fisch
(*feesh*)
fish

eine Zeitung
(*eye-na tsight-oong*)
a newspaper

Spielzeuge
(*shpeel-tsoiga*)
toys

Marmelade
(*marmelarda*)
jam

eins (*eye-nce*) one

zwei (*tsv-eye*) two

drei (*dry*) three

vier (*fear*) four

fünf (*funf*) five

sechs (*zex*) six

sieben (*zeeben*) seven

acht (*akht*) eight

neun (*noin*) nine

zehn (*tsayn*) ten

 Schwarz (*shvarts*) black

 weiß (*vice*) white

 rot (*rote*) red

 gelb (*gelp*) yellow

 grün (*grewn*) green

 blau (*bl-ow*) blue

 Montag (*Moan-targ*) Monday

 Dienstag (*Deens-targ*) Tuesday

Januar (*Yanoo-ar*) January

Februar (*Feb-rew-ar*) February

März (*Mairts*) March

April (*Apreel*) April

Mai (*My*) May

Juni (*Yoonee*) June

Juli (*Yoolee*) July

August (*Owgust*) August

September (*Zeptember*) September

Oktober (*October*) October

November (*November*) November

 **Mittwoch** (*Mittvokh*) Wednesday

Donnerstag (*Donners-targ*) Thursday

Freitag (*Fry-targ*) Friday

Samstag (*Zams-targ*) Saturday

Sonntag (*Zoon-targ*) Sunday

Dezember (*Detsember*) December